Revealing

Unto the World, Bring Forth

Clarity to Life,

Who We Really Are, From Where Do We Come & What Is Our Purpose

(DNA Bloodlines/Genetic Compass, Can Be Partial Answers For Some?)

R. E. VINCENT DANIELS

Outskirts Press, Inc.
http://www.outskirtspress.com

ISBN: 978-1-9772-7464-9

Cover Photo © 2024 R. E. Vincent Daniels. All rights reserved - used with permission.

Outskirts Press and the "OP" logo are trademarks belonging to Outskirts Press, Inc.

PRINTED IN THE UNITED STATES OF AMERICA

TABLE OF CONTENTS

FOREWORD

"A Fictional Graphic Novel, Encapsulating Historical Facts (FGNEHF)"

Stephen Hawking:"The Secret of Our Identity is in the Past"

"It's the past that tells us what we are, and Where We're From, without it, there is no identity to speak of."

"Self Realization of One's Historical Identity"

"Shattering The Myth, And Conquering the Fear, Going Where, few if any, Others Dare to Ever Venture!

"Bring Forth an Historical Truth Paradigm,
Replacing Cultural/Societal Paradox,
Myths, Lies and Stereotypes; Setting
the Records Straight."

"Reclaiming a Historical Heritage, by Destroying
False Myths; Truth will Then Empower"

"Whoever Control the Present, will Control
the Narrative of Past Historical Facts"

"At some point in the lives of us all, during the human journey, the Past will Become One's Presents in Time. It is our heritage and DNA that dictates much of what we are to become in life, in conjunction with experiences along the way, but we do have some control of our life journey as well, based on choices made or not!"

Any and all attempts to appropriate and/or erase the Greatness of the African peoples has failed, because truth will never surrender to lies, but only lay siege to destroy the myths that propitiates the quest for the powers associated with supremacy over the other! History, if true, has so many lessons to teach us, given the proper exposure to the general public. Just that dynamic, would most likely bring about a significance humanitarian difference to the lives we would be allowed to experience. Institutional amnesia, can never be allowed to govern the teaching of truth and verifiable historical facts and data, as they relate to the greatness of the humanity of the peoples of African heritage, who have played a significant role in the global evolution of all mankind!

Author's Bio

R. E. Vincent Daniels
BS. & MS. STEM College Degrees & several Certifications

Born and raised in Bedford Stuyvesant community in Brooklyn, NYC, in the times of segregation/American Apartheid, that in large part, still persists in these United States of American, in the 21st century, even thought it has manifested itself in different fashions over the years, I.E. Book Banning and Critical Race Theory (CRT). I am concerned that Americans are stuck in a racial muck, but seeks to double down, now making it Quick Sand into Cement, so things will revert back to its ugly radical racist past.

I am a parent of three and a grandparent of three, four boys and two girls of African decent. The adult children all are products of a public school system with standardized curriculum and syllabus which is geared toward a Eurocentric inferences, associated with perceived supremacy. The theme of this book projects, is the global perspective of the peoples of both African and Chinese heritage. How amazing is it, that the original peoples African, globally established the foundation for the civilization of all mankind on planet Earth, such as in China! The facts that confirm the STEM/STEAMM (Science, Technology, Engineering, Art, Mathematics & Medicine) skillset for the world, was and is so very spectacular in and of its self, is owed to African peoples! Perhaps this work will help disbelievers, to begin to rethink the perceived notions, that the academic and intellectual institutions has taught for centuries, is in fact based, in large part, on Western propergander and false data, projecting a perceived supremacy over the other!

Whenever one reads my works, do so with an open mind; never going in with the luggage/baggage of past thoughts and ideas, acquired from past exposures! Letting facts and data govern your thought patterns and understanding. And then, remember to always fact check, on your own, everything you have been told or were taught going forward; even what appears in my writings as well! This will require effort, but it will be worth the time spent and one can then be truly informed and educated! With what you will have learned, you must share with all others, paying it forward, by being a disciple of legitimate academic and intellectual truths, based on verifiable facts and associated data points!

DEDICATION

Driven by the ancestral presents of my Mom, Edna Vincent Daniels; my Dad, Philip G. Oats Daniels Jr.; my Grandmother, Bertha Oats Daniels; and now my wife, Ms Darlene T. Cherry Daniels. I continue to pursue the historical facts, stolen from African peoples and for the most part, from the entire world. It is my childhood experiences, that encourage me on this quest, to help make future generations, like my three grandchildren, to be that much better off. My mom and dad made it better for my brother, Norman(Nat) and myself, therefore it is imperative, that I, carryon that very tradition, having received the baton, in the relay of life. This project is my ongoing effort, doing what is embedded in my DNA. It is my hope, that all my works, will inspire others, to take up a similar mantels in their own way? To do such, in order to make this world a better place, than the one we were born into!

BOOK INTRODUCTION

At some point in our lives, we should seek to learn about those family members who preceded us; setting the ground work and foundation we were born into this world. One such person is Chee Luang, a young Chinese woman, living in New York City, that wondered about her family heritage? She had explored the subject back in grade school; driven by a class assignment from her teacher Ms M., which required each student to research their family homeland of origin, and then report their findings to the class.

It was her African American classmates, the

T & T Washington Twins, Tiye and Tarik, who stole the show, with their extensive and detailed research results, about documenting, little known facts, of the peoples of Africa. Their verifiable data and facts, which were not easy to find, supported their final report. The school and local libraries didn't carry adequate resources, that could be used for the class project? They resorted to the library on the campus of Howard University, an HBC (Historical Black College) and the internet, to obtain the required data and facts. Their project was so outstanding, the Twins were encouraged to give a school assembly program presentation, on their report results. Chee, had then, relied on her parent's recollections of her family's Chinese historical stories, which by the way, were somewhat limited and vague, due to their lack of documented data; the library sources, were also very superficial in their coverage of Chinese history?

Fast forward, Chee, as a Pre Med student at a prestigious university, like Columbia University, now wanted more information and resorted to the popular services of "Ancestry" resources, to fill in the obvious gaps, from her past grade school classroom assignment. It is the unexpected results, of that ancestral search, which sets the stage of the intriguing family historical foundation, which then launched Chee's desire to fact check, from whence she came, a ancient Chinese Dynasty. This would played a significant role in the establishment of her mysterious Chinese cultural heritage? Like all Asian cultures, there is the intriguing and magical vibe, that is often conveyed, in the stories that surround the culture and religious beliefs of them all? Now share Chee's Luang family discovery and how she copes with something she didn't expect to find; how it formulate her personality and thoughts, about her true history, along with the history of the world. It is factual history, that will brings about a real reclamation, which can truly alter the paradigm, that governs behavior and cultural realities of each of us, as well as how the global population perceives one's significance and relevance in the timeline of historical facts of humanity!

Chapter 1

Chapter 1

CHEE LUANG RECOGNITION
AND ACKNOWLEDGEMENT

SAY HI AGAIN to Chee Luang, years later, after our initial meeting in the Brooklyn Heights classroom, of teacher Ms M(McNamara). For clarification it was first in the book, "See Us, From Whence We Come". It was where the T&T Twins, Tiye and Tarik, discover their true African greatness, initiated by the completion of a class assignment, to define the family homeland and associated historical background.

Full disclosure, it was the sharing of the vast knowledge the twins uncovered, from their extensive research, aided by parents and grandparents, that enlightened the students of African greatness, often omitted and/or appropriated by society and academic institutions globally.

Chee, in pursuit of her family's history and land of birth, had in the past, only skimmed the surface, due to the limited knowledge from family members and available tainted written archives, that only provided a standardized European recollection of the greatness of Chinese History.

With the pasting of time, Chee Luang has matured to quite a

young woman of accomplishments. She had gone onto complete high school with honors, both with high SAT and ACT grades, which in turn, opened up doors of higher education, that her family would not normally be able to afford. Several Ivey league Universities had pursued her, with offers of grants and student work programs. She had decided in High School on a career in the Medical Field, whether it be in Research or Practical disciplines? In the end, it was Columbia University that she finally selected, with the thought in mind, to still be close to home and the family she so enjoyed; she was very attached to, her family, as is the typical Asia tradition?

Chee had two younger siblings to help raise and set a positive example for; that, along with other family concerns, played a major role in the selection of Columbia, as her college of choice. Chinese/Asian cultural traditions, were a very strong influence in her conciseness and sense of societal responsibilities. She was very aware of the American history of the Chinese being recruited to build the western railroads, so many years ago. How the Chinese were treated, once the railroad were completed, and how they are treated in current times; the stereo typical, some positive and negative in nature. In America, ethnics are very often tainted with stereo typical characterizations? That made her super aware of her need to supersede, all barriers society had put in place, based on her proud Chinese heritage.

The neighborhood she resided in was predominantly populated with peoples of Asian backgrounds, such as Japanese, Koreans, and some Vietnamese. New York City had large populations of Asian peoples in the lower east side in Manhattan and in Flushing Queen. Chee had friends and classmates from both communities, which allowed her to had shared experiences, with folks of like backgrounds and heritages; shared holidays and foods, that were so very familiar to her. The various Asian cultures mirrored each other, in so many ways. It was that familiarity, that emboldened her. Back in her primary school up bringing, there weren't that many Asian peoples sharing that space, however the multicultural experiences were also very valuable to Chee,

Revealing Unto the World, Bring Forth Clarity to Life, Who We Really Are, From Where do We Come & What Is Our Purpose

she learned about the numerous cultures, she had the fortune to inter-
act with. It was the African American interaction with the T&T Twins,
Tiye and Tarik, that left the greatest impression on Chee, too this day!
She did in fact, missed the two of them the most!

Chapter 2

DESIRE TO CONNECT WITH
HER CHINESE LEGACY

WITH SO MUCH happening in her life, Chee had made a promise to her mom and dad, she would one day make a return visit to their family homeland of China. The politics, being what they are, China being communist and America democratic politically, the dichotomy was so obvious, yet she still wanted, somehow to make the trip, when and if the opportunity presented itself. As faith would have it, the chance to make the Chinese visit, did in fact present itself.

Chee was going into her sophomore year, in Pre Med studies, at Colombia University, when an exchange program was introduced, for medical students to spend a semester in a foreign country, China was one of the options available to students? Over whelmed by this opportunity, to visit China, which was a lifetime dream of her's. It was like her dream request was answered by fate?

She had to qualify for the available position, in order to be chosen for such an adventurous trip. Having just entering her second year of studies, she had to get her grade point average up, in order to satisfy the required A+ qualifying mark for selection. Chee knew, she needed to get serious about her education at that point, it is because of her selected area of studies, that this opportunity had come to her door step, but she had to do better academically, in order to qualify for the exchange semester in China.

She went home to inform her family, letting them know of the possible good fortune, that might come her way, only if she got her grades up, so she could be illegible. Her mom and dad, were so happy for her and promised to assist her in the quest to bring her grades up. It was her sister and brother both, also wanting the best for Chee and promised to not get in the way of her studies, so her grades could improve to the A+ level.

From September on, in the first half of her sophomore year of studies, Chee spent endless hours in the library and study sessions with fellow students, so her grades would improve; she sort help, when necessary, from the smartest students in her various classes, to glean the knowledge for the test and class projects. At the end of the Fall semester, she had only improved her over all grade level to a mark of an A, but she needed that little bit extra, in order reach that A+ level. The Spring Semester would require just that extra level effort to makeup for the A grade average she had obtained, during her freshman year of studies. Back to work this time, during the Spring semester, which meant, no social life on the weekends and long days and nights back in the library. If necessary she would do extra project work for the professors? Chee's classmates and friends would never see her outside the classroom and/ or the library. Her weekends were spent with her head in the books and her study days were eighteen or more hours long, twenty four seven!

When the Spring semester ended, Chee crossed her fingers that she would have reached her goal? As fate would have it; she had lost some friendships and a potential boyfriend, who was no longer interested in her company, yet it turned out, she, had in fact achieved her overall grade point goal of an A+. It turned out that her sacrifice, had indeed paid off! The selection committee had observed Chee all along, during her sophomore year and admired the effort, dedication and sacrifices she had made, in order to achieve her goal and would had selected her, no matter what, the final grade point average turned out to be? She had exemplified the desire and hard work, which merited her selection, by the way, she in fact, was the last student to be chosen for the overseas exchange study program to China. When Chee was informed in June, she shared the great news with her family and all rejoiced in her achievement!

She couldn't believe it, she was on the way to China in the fall and would room with a Chinese student, well versed in both, English and Chinese languages, so her transition would be made easier.

Chapter 3

DISCOVERY OF AFRICAN HERITAGE

THE SUMMER MONTHS of July and August were spent in preparation for this momentous trip. She want to be well prepare for the experience, so she decided to get her Ancestral DNA check back in March of the Spring semester. When the resulted came back, she was somewhat surprised and amazed, by the fact the data indicated, she had 20% African heredity. This came as a shock for Chee, her mom and dad alike? They knew the family had royal leakage to the ancient Shang Dynasty, the first dynasty of Chinese history, but no knowledge of the origin of the peoples who built it?.

(The Shang dynasty, the first historically confirmed kingdom, supposedly started when the Shang overthrew the Xia sometime about the time period of 1760 BCE (Before the Common Era). The Mythical Period was deemed very earliest time of traditional Chinese history according to legendary beliefs, Xia dynasty ruled China. The Shang ruled the Yellow River Valley for the majority of the second millennium, approximately from 1766 to 1046 BCE.)—[Source Credit A & B noted later.])

It was the family elders, who had informed her that the family Luang, were from a small remote village in a province, fin northeastern region of the Chinese countryside, not far from the historical Yellow River Valley of China. The Luang's were thought to be somewhat connected, family wise, with the royal family of the Shang rulers? Elders had vague details of the so call family relationship and ties to the Shang Dynasty?

It was Chee's hopes, that her visit to China would allow her time to further investigate this ancient connection, to the Shang rulers of the first Chinese recorded dynasty, because to her thinking, it was there, where the African linkage might well had taken place? This of course, would most likely be a very long shoot, but more than worth trying to pin down the family connection, after thousands of years. Many family connections, very well, would be uncovered in the search and therefore will result in positive information, for her family to have knowledge of?

Chapter 4

REACHING OUT FOR CLARIFICATION

HAVING RECEIVED THIS mind changing news, Chee was forced to recall, her Ms M. classroom assignment, to report on the family heritage and homeland, years before. The fact the she was part African, never materialized, because the family elders were also, not aware as well? Chee needed clarification and further understanding; her thoughts flashed back to the T&T Twins, her close African American classmates and friends from the past.

By means of a social media internet search, Chee located the contact information on the T&T Twins, Tiye and Tarik. They still resided in Brooklyn Heights. They were attending NYU University and studying, you guessed it, to become College Professors in global historical disciplines, concentrating on African historical studies. When Chee called, both Tiye and Tarik we're so excited to reconnect with her, after so many years had elapsed and they all had gone their individual ways. After the several moments of exchanging pleasantries and catching up over the phone, Chee explained why she sort their counsel on African historical facts and her recent Ancestry DNA results. The initial response by the twins, was to meet up in person, to discuss a strategy to address Chee's curiosity?

Upon meeting in a coffee shop, close to NYU in the Villages, the strategy agreed upon, was to pursue the greater knowledge of the African historian professors on campus, in order to define the sources of the linkage to Chee's African connection! With permission of the NYU Historical Department and the very learned professors on staff, the three old classmates began their research, after being pointed in the right directions by the learned instructors. They were told that the internet was the best source, for the most up to date facts, because African historical facts and data was often hidden or appropriated, by most of the Western historical scholars; there were some exceptions, along with African American historians, who have written on the subject matter, the historical Moorish/Chinese connectivity.

After delaying the start of the historical search, until after their spring semesters completed, so as not to distract from their individual studies, they all agreed to meet up in late June or early July, to kickoff the historical search for the Chinese/African relationship. In the mean time, Chee was informed of her acceptance in the Chinese/American Columbia University student exchange program, for her junior Fall Semesters.

Between keeping up her grades overseas, Chee knew, she needed to get as much historical information available documented and recorded over the summer months, preceding her trip to China? The trio got together in late June, to begin the research process and data recording. They utilized the library facilities of both NYU and Columbia Universities, in conjunction with the American Museum of Natural History archives. All three academic archives are classified as world class, and were locally available. The resources of the internet were of value as well and could be accessed at their home base. The trio were in constant contact, comparing notes and documenting data, so as to minimize duplication of dates and facts.

This intense academic ancestral research was conducted none stop, for the better part of two months times, while taking the weekends off, not to consume their entire summer break. Remembering, Chee had sacrificed her social life, the five months previously, but this was still her priority and time was so very tight. The Twins would not have given up their break time, for anyone else, other than Chee, because they were so close and they were aware, that the data would likely mean so much, to her and her family, like their own research, was life changing for them, so many year before. It in fact, set the career path for the Twins, as they pursued teaching professions to make a difference in lives of the future generations of students to come, in the African Diaspora, as well as with all students globally, here to for, deprived of truth of African Historical greatness, in the greater pursuit of legitimate academic and intellectual acquisition of knowledge! Chee Luang journey, would be much akin, to the journey of the Washington Twins, so many years before? In the African tradition, known as "Sankofa*", the looking back in order to go forward!

(***Sankofa** is a word in the <u>Twi language</u> of <u>Ghana</u> that translates to "Go back and get it" (*san*—to return; *ko*—to go; *fa*—to fetch, to seek and take) and also refers to the <u>Asante</u> <u>Adinkrasymbol</u> represented either with a stylized heart shape or by a bird with its head turned backwards while its feet face forward carrying a precious egg in its mouth. Sankofa is often associated with the proverb, "*Se wo were fi na wosankofa a yenkyi*," which translates as: "It is not wrong to go back for that which you have forgotten."[1])

(What is the following, is the chapter on the sum total of the documented academic data/facts collected and categorized by the trio over the two month summer period of time, with appropriate reference sources so noted. The final document was to accompany Chee on her overseas Chinese journey.)

Chapter 5

RESEARCH AND CONFIRMATION
GOING FORWARD

DOCUMENTED HISTORICAL RESEARCH and Confirmation Data, collected and categorized by the trio going forward, associated reference source credits (A & B), are therefore legitimately noted as such in the text:

DATA SUMMARY:

African Moors in Asia/Orient (China/Japan/India) interaction over a millennium of time. Some use the two terms, Asia and Orient interchangeably; a definition of each term will be provided in the text to follow for some clarification. Should then become apparent that the two don't represent the same regions on the globe, with slight nuances!

A. ASIA DEFINED:

Asia is the world's largest and most populous world continent, covering approximately 44.58 million square kilometers and home to over

4.5 billion people. It is located primarily in the eastern hemisphere of the globe and is bordered by the Arctic Ocean to the north, the Pacific Ocean to the east, the Indian Ocean to the south, and Europe to the west. Asia is known for its many diverse cultures, religions, and languages, with countries such as China, India, Japan, and Russia being some of the most prominent.

THE FIRST CHINESE PEOPLE

The Shang Dynasty is the earliest ruling dynasty of China to be established in recorded history, though other dynasties predated it. The Shang ruled from 1600 to 1046 B.C. and heralded the Bronze Age in China. They were known for their advances in math, astronomy, artwork and military technology.

BEGINNING OF THE SHANG DYNASTY

The earliest written records in Chinese history date back to the Shang Dynasty, which, according to legend, began when a tribal chief named Tang defeated the Xia Dynasty, which in 1600 B.C. was under the control of a tyrant named Jie. This victory is known as the Battle of Mingtiao, fought during a thunderstorm. Jie survived the battle but died later of illness. Tang is known for establishing a low number of drafted soldiers in the army and for beginning social programs to help the kingdom's poor.Shang Dynasty Achievements People of the Shang Dynasty are believed to have used calendars and developed knowledge of astronomy and math, thanks to inscriptions on tortoise shell that have been unearthed by archaeologists. The Shang calendar was at first lunar-based, but a solar-based one was developed by a man named Wan-Nien, who established a 365-day year through his observations and pinpointed the two solstices. Shang Dynasty artisans created sophisticated bronze works, ceramics and trinkets made from jade. Unlike their Bronze Age counterparts, artisans during the Shang Dynasty used piece-mold casting as opposed to the lost-wax method. This meant that they first made a model of the object they wanted to create before covering it in a clay mold. The clay mold would then be cut into sections, removed and re-fired to create a new, unified one. By 1200 B.C., Shang armies were equipped with horse-drawn chariots. Before that, there is evidence of bronze-tipped spears, halberds (pointed axes) and bows. The language of the Shang Dynasty is an early form of modern Chinese. Chinese characters first appeared during the Shang Dynasty inscribed on cattle bone and tortoise shells. There is evidence of two numerological systems, one based on numbers from one to 10 and the other from one to 12.

FIRST CHINESE DYNASTY

The very earliest period in traditional Chinese history is called the **Mythical Period**, when—according to legend—the **Xia dynasty** ruled China. The **Shang dynasty**, the first historically confirmed dynasty, supposedly began when the Shang overthrew the Xia sometime around 1760 BCE.

Did this overthrow actually happen? We're not sure. The Shang dynasty is the oldest Chinese dynasty whose existence is supported by archaeological finds, but more evidence for the existence of the Xia dynasty may yet emerge.

It's estimated that the Shang ruled the Yellow River Valley of China for most of the second millennium BCE—so about 1766 to 1046 BCE.

What of the African presence in early China? Have there been Black people in China? If so, what became of them? What happened to the Black people of early China? Are they still there? These are profound questions. Indeed, the African presence in China is perhaps the most challenging area of research within the broad realm of the African presence in Asia. Challenging though it may be, however, it is not an area that can be dismisse

Chancellor Williams, for example, in his classic Destruction of Black Civilization, noted that:

"Ancient China and the Far East, for example, must be a special area of African research. How do we explain such a large population of Blacks in southern China, powerful enough to form a kingdom of their own?" While in September 1998, a scientific study posted in the Los Angeles Times concluded that:

"A significant number, if not most, of the population of modern China—one fifth or more of all people living today—owes it's genetic origins to Africa."

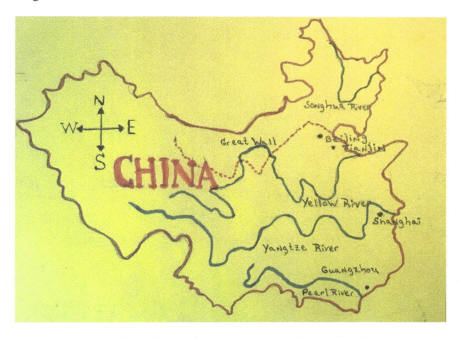

From the realm of the physical anthropology of early China, according to the preeminent scholar in the field, Kwan-chih Chang:

"Skeletal remains from the Hoabinhian and Bacsoinan strata, similar to those found in southwest China, bear Oceanic Negroids features." The first Black people in China then—the people who are probably the first of any people in China—were apparently Black people akin to the Batwa of Central Africa and the people of the Andaman Islands today—we call the Diminutive Africoids. They survived well into the historical periods.

The presence of Diminutive Africoids (whom Chinese historians called Black Dwarfs) in early southern China during the period of the Three Kingdoms (ca. 250 CE) is recorded in the book of the Official of the Liang Dynasty (502-556 CE).

They are said to be Diminutive Africoids and are variously called Pygmies, Negritos and Aeta. They are found in the Philippines, northern Malaysia, Thailand, Sumatra in Indonesia and other places.

Chinese historians called them "Black dwarfs" in the Three Kingdoms period (AD 220 to AD 280) and they were still to be found in China during the Qing dynasty (1644 to 1911). In Taiwan they were called the "little Black people" and, apart from being diminutive, they were also said to be broad-nosed and dark-skinned with curly hair.

These Diminutive Africoids inhabit the Andaman Islands, a remote archipelago east of India, and are direct descendants of the first modern humans to have inhabited Asia, geneticists conclude in new studies.

Their physical features, short stature, dark skin, peppercorn hair and large buttocks are characteristic of so-called African "Pygmies." Only four of the numerous groups that once inhabited the Andamans survive, with a total population of about 500 people. These include the Jarawa, who still live in the forest, and the Onge, who have been settled there by the Indian government.

By Dr. Clyde WintersEdited by Ogu-Eji-Ofo-Annu

It can be reasonably assumed that the first inhabitants of the chinese mainland were Black Brown Africans from East, West and Central regions of Africa given that the earliest human skeletal remains in China are of "Negro" (or â€œNegritosâ€ a psuedo-scientific term commonly used today) people. The next oldest skeletal type after the period of predominance of the African immigrants were the Classical Mongoloids or Austronesian speakers.

Archaeological research makes it clear that "Negroids" (read: Central African skeletal types) were very common to ancient China.

F. Weidenreich in Bull. Nat. Hist. Soc. Peiping 13, (1938-30) noted that the one of the earliest skulls from north China found in the Upper Cave of Chou-k'ou-tien, was of a Oceanic Negroid/ Melanesoid " (p.163). This is the so-called Peking Man. This would place people in China during the Mesolithic looking like African/Negro people , not native American.

These Blacks were the dominant group in South China. Kwang-chih Chang, writing in the 4th edition of Archaeology of ancient China (1986) wrote that:" by the beginning of the Recent (Holocene) period the population in North China and that in the southwest and in Indochina had become sufficiently differentiated to be designated as Mongoloid and OCEANIC NEGROID races respectivelyâ€¦."(p.64). By the Upper Pleistocene the Negroid type was typified by the Liu-chiang skulls from Yunnan (Chang, 1986, p.69).

Negroid skeletons dating to the early periods of Southern Chinese history have been found in Shangdong, Jiantung, Sichuan, Yunnan, Pearl River delta and Jiangxi especially at the initial sites of Chingliengang (Ch'ing-lien-kang) and Mazhiabang (Ma chia-pang) phases (see: K.C. Chang, The archaeology of ancient China, (Yale University Press:New Haven,1977) p.76) . The Chingliengang culture is often referred to as the Ta-wen-k'ou (Dawenkou) culture of North China. The presence of Negroid skeletal remains at Dawenkou sites make it clear that Negroes spread out from the North to South China. The Dawenkou culture predates the Lung-shan culture which is associated with the Xia civilization.

Many researchers believe that the Yi of Southern China were the ancestors of the Austronesian, Polynesian and Melanesian people.

In the Chinese literature the Blacks were called li-min, Kunlung, Ch'iang (Qiang), Yi and Yueh. The founders of the Xia Dynasty and the Shang Dynasties were blacks. These blacks were called Yueh and Qiang. The modern Chinese are descendants of the Zhou. The second Shang Dynasty (situated at Anyang) was founded by the Yin. As a result this dynasty is called Shang-Yin.

The Yin or Classical/Oceanic Mongoloid type is associated with the Austronesian speakers (Kwang-chih Chang, "Prehistoric and early historic culture horizons and traditions in South China", Current Anthropology, 5 (1964) pp.359-375 :375). Djehuti your Austronesian or Oceanic ancestors were referred to in the Chinese literature as Yin, Feng, Yen, Zhiu Yi and Lun Yi.

It is not clear that contemporary European and Chinese people are descendants of the original Black population which lived in Europe and Asia; neither is it clear that the Chinese are descendants of the Austronesian speaking people.

Textual evidence and the skeletal record seem to indicate that contemporary Chinese and European people come out of nowhere after 1500 BC, the European Sea People came from the North and attacked Egypt, and the Chinese (Hua) people came from the North and ran the Black Qiang and Yueh tribes, along with the Austronesian Yin (classical mongoloid or Austronesian speakers) off the Chinese mainland back into Southeast Asia or on to the Pacific Islands.

SOURCES: A

Chang, Kwan-chih. The Archaeology of Ancient China. New Haven: Yale University Press, 1963.
Chi, Li. The Formation of the Chinese People: An Anthropological Inquiry. 1928; rpt. New York: Russell and Russell, 1967.
Komaroff, Linda. Gifts of the Sultan. New Haven: Los Angeles County Museum of Art, Yale University Press, 2011.
Quartly, Jules. The Taipei Times, Nov. 27, 2004.
Rogers, J.A. Sex and Race, vol. 1. St. Petersburg: Helga M. Rogers, 1968.
The Los Angeles Times, Sept. 29, 1998.
Williams, Chancellor. The Destruction of Black Civilization.

B. MOORS OF THE ORIENT

The Japanese, Chinese, Aryans and people of India are direct descendants of the Moors

The Orient Defined:

However the term "Orient" refers to the region of the world that includes countries in East and Southeast Asia, including China, Japan, Korea, Vietnam, and Thailand specifically. The term was originally a term made popular by Europeans to refer to the countries and cultures of this region, which were seen as exotic and mysterious.

(Take note, that Russia is not included in this definition!)

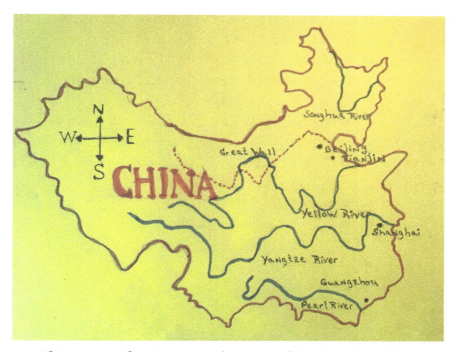

Africans were first in Asia and pioneered Asia's early civilization!

The Africans Moors role in Asia as elsewhere in the world has been submerged and distorted for centuries. Asia's African roots are well summarized in African Presence in Early Asia by Ivan Van Sertima

& Runoko Rashidi, and African Presence in Early China by James Brunson.

The original oriental people were moors referred to as Black people in North America, and many of them still are Dark of Hue complexion—southern China and Asia. The earliest occupants of Asia were 'small 'Blacks' (at times you may see the work Black in quotes so that you continue to have an idea of whom Iâ€™m addressing) (pygmies) who came to the region as early as 50,000 years ago Christian Calendar **(Keep in mind that the Romans added 580 years to the Moorish Calendar, Now tell me, if you defeated or colonized a nation would you not mark your beginning of your rule, change their names, culture and belief system, well yes, that also included the calendar).**

In 100 Amazing Facts About The Negro, J.A. Rogers reports that in 1923, Europeans first discovered "a hitherto unknown Negro race, the Nakhis, 200,000 in number, in Southern China." **(Yes your mind went through a mental zone because the word Negro was used. I must now reveal to you that the word Negro derives from a river, please read 100 Amazing facts. It was the miss-education and the prejudice instilled in us that had us believe other wise. However, in North America it has been accepted as a derogatory word, therefore, I recommend to not use it due to the history that was practiced its use)** In The Children of the Sun George Parker writes "… it appears that the entire continent of Asia was originally the home of many 'black' people and that these people were the pioneers in establishing the wonderful civilizations that have flourished throughout this vast continent." The Premier have learned that we were the Asiatic people and this was the name of the entire planet before a continent was called Africa, and that we were the original people of the land. If you take a closer look you will realize that Asia is bigger than the portion that is now called Africa, and that you can fit Africa in Asiatic. Also all must remember that there was NO European continent during Moorish rule, they renamed the land mass, just like Columbus called the Moors Trinidadians because he saw three mountains.

The question is what did they call themselves? Reports of major kingdoms ruled by Moors are frequent in Chinese documents. The first kingdom of Southeast Asia is called Fou Nan, famous for building masterful canal systems. Chinese historians described the Fou Nanese men as "small and black." The Ainus, Japan's oldest known inhabitants, have traditions which tell of a race of dark dwarfs which inhabited **Japan before they did (if you read the Clock of Destiny Book 2 you will understand that the Japanese are Moors as well).** Historians Cheikh Anta Diop and Albert Churchward saw the Ainus as originating in Egypt! There is archeological support for this. In addition, ancient Egypt and Mesopotamia records the "Anu" (Ainu?). The Ainu "... are of the same original race and type as the Australian Aborigines" reports Churchward in Signs and Symbols of Primordial Man. J.A. Rogers writes in Sex and Race Vol. I, "... there are many numbers of Japanese who, but for color and hair, bear a striking resemblance to the South African Bushman..." An ancient tradition points to the conquest of Japan from the southeast by a race of Black warriors.

Did Africans build those ancient pyramids in Japan and China?

There are man-made pyramids in China and Japan! China's pyramids are located near Siang Fu city in the Shensi province. The Chinese do not know how they got there but it is believed that Africans of the Nile Valley were the builders (J. Perry: The Growth of Civilization p.106,107) Mistaken for hill due to there eroded appearance; the ones in Japan are made of stones not indigenous to Japan. It is said they were built during the time of Mu. (see page 15) (A. Tebecis: Mahikari—Thank God for the Answers at Last—at Mahikari Centers, LA **(310) 316-6867**, The Pyramids of Japan—film by Alpha Media Corp.)

China's first historical dynasty and first emperor were Moors (Black Africans)!

Founded by King Tang or Ta, the earliest documented rulership of China was the Shang Dynasty (or Chiang) c. 1500-1000 B.C., which is credited with bringing together the elements of China's earliest known civilization. **The Shang were given the name Nakhi (Na-Black,**

Khi-man). Under the Black dynasty, the Chinese established the basic forms of a graceful calligraphy that has lasted to the present day. **The first Chinese emperor, the legendary Fu-Hsi (2953-2838** B.C.— before the colonization of the moors) was a wooly haired Black Man. He is credited with establishing government, originating social institutions and cultural inventions. He is said to have originated the I Ching, or The Book of Change, which is the oldest, most revered system of **prophecy. It is known to have influenced the most distinguished philosophers of Chinese thought.**

The martial arts originated in what they call AFRICA, not Asia!

Kilindi Iyi's essay in African Presence in Early Asia (by Van Sertima/ Rashidi) reveals the African roots of the martial arts: Africans discovered very early that the movements of animals could be used effectively to develop their fighting skills. Also, that 'animal principles' could be isolated within the consciousness and manifested into an unconquerable fighting force. **The oldest records of kicking, throwing, wrestling, and punching techniques were found in Egypt. These warrior scientists laid the foundation for all martial arts systems, including Kung Fu and Judo.**

The first people of India were Africans (Moors)! The word India itself means Black. Yoga and other so-called Eastern teachings originated in Africa!

The Latin word "India" is from the Greek word Indus (or Indos) which means Black. The earliest people of India were â€˜Blackâ€™ Africans, Who do you think built the Tag Mahall(! It is believed that many of them came from Ethiopia. Often called Dravidians, these Moors founded the great Indus Valley Civilization around 3000 B.C. They brought with them many spiritual sciences which originated in Africa, such as those of Yoga, Kundalini and Reflexology. They were masters of urban planning and architecture: their homes and cities had running water, toilets, and an underground sewage system!—evidenced at the Mohenjo Daro ruins (2000 B.C.). It is believed that the Ganges, the sacred river of India, is named after an Ethiopian king of

Revealing Unto the World, Bring Forth Clarity to Life, Who We Really Are, From Where do We Come & What Is Our Purpose

that name who conquered Asia as far as this river. Buddha, Krishna, and other great Black sages arose from their successive civilizations, including the great King Asoka.

Barbaric whites invaded India, bringing destruction.

Around the 7th century B.C., nomadic, barbaric tribes of whites invaded India. Like their Greek cousins were to do later, these uncivilized whites learned civilization from the Moors and overthrew them, destroying their great civilization. Like their European cousins were to do later with Christianity and Judaism, they distorted the â€˜Black'sâ€™ religion and spiritual values into a system which ensured their superiority while suppressing the natives (**look today at the white jesus in many homes of dark and fair complexion Moorish homes, referred to as Africans, West Indians, Dominicans, Cubans, Japanese etc).** The caste system is the basis of their cunning, oppressive religious ideology which to this day enslaves the mind, body and soul of indigenous Blacks. Originally called Brahminism, this religion was altered and is now called Hinduism—the greatest curse to India's Blacks. According to Madame Blavatsky—founder of Theosophy and a woman mason (a philosophy based on India's sacred sciences and Moorish Sufism), a type of caste system was already in place before the â€˜whitesâ€™ arrived. They got worst and exploited it, putting themselves on top. Historians incorrectly refer to these whites as "Aryan," a word stolen from the Sanskrit language of India's Blacks, where it meant noble cultivator or the holy as a title for Rishis (sages) who mastered the sacred science of Aryasatyani. Yes, we were called the Aryan nation, but the ignorance of many little European children they once again stole the rights and turned it into and supreme power and distaste for themselves and against the people that are the founders of it.

No justice exists for the Dalits: India's Black "Untouchables".

At the top of the Hindu caste pyramid sits the Brahmin. At the bottom are the heavily exploited, degraded, humiliated, slave-like, impoverished "Untouchables" who carry the weight of the entire population. They are the worse victims of Hindu society, along with women at all caste levels. African Presence in Early Asia presents an essay by Indian activists T. Rajshekar who writes: "From the very beginning it [Brahminism/Hinduism] has had the suppression of the native population and women, even Aryan women, as its primary principles… whereas the natives respected all humans and assured equal status to women. **In fact, the natives of India were matriarchal…**" These Moorish Untouchables are the long-suffering descendants of Aryan/Black unions and native Moorish populations who retreated into the hinterlands of India seeking escape from the advancing Aryan influence under which they eventually succumbed. They call themselves Dalits which means crushed and broken. Though the caste system (or varna system) was based originally on skin color (varna means color), color is not the main problem as some dark or light skinned people are found at the top and bottom. The problem is the sanctioned oppression of Moorish Untouchables. No justice exists for them! Crimes against them by caste Hindus almost always go unpunished! Rajshekar writes

"No where else in the world is there a parallel to the Aryan persecution of the untouchables of India… It is a social, cultural, and religious institution… The caste structure maintains itself because every member of a particular caste group stands to gain by belonging to that particular caste-group. The caste system helps the exploitation of the weak by the strong. India's constitution not only does not interfere with caste, but fully upholds it… Caste system is based on purity and pollution. One group is considered more pure than the other. The less pure caste group accepts its lower status because it is happy that it has a much larger caste group below it to exploit. As long as there is somebody below it to exploit, it is proud and will not mind somebody always standing on its shoulders. So the entire caste structure is a … self-sustaining, automatic, exploitive machine."

India's â€˜Blacksâ€™ are ignorant of their Moorish roots.

India's native Moorish population is the largest Moorish population outside Africa, numbering about 200 million. They have brown

Revealing Unto the World, Bring Forth Clarity to Life, Who We Really Are, From Where do We Come & What Is Our Purpose

to black skin, straight or kinky hair and African features, such as the famous Indian holy man, Sathya Sai Baba who has a large **kinky afro. Rajshekar writes "The Black untouchables of India, even the educated among them are not aware of the common origin of Africans and Dalits. Would you not say the same applies to your Parrish or country?**

When they come to know of this and the struggle of the moors referred to as African-Americans and their spectacular achievements, our people will naturally become proud. **Putting pride into their broken hearts is our prime task...** This is why the Clock of Destiny Moorish International Order of the Great Seal encourages the Asiatics to read certain books. The Moorish-Americans (That means South America, North America and Central America also must know that their liberation struggle cannot be complete as long as their own bloodbrothers and sisters living in far off Asia are suffering. It is true that Moors and India's Black Untouchables better know as moors are both the victims of racism...American leaders can give our struggle tremendous support by bringing forth knowledge of the existence of such a huge chunk of Asian Moors to the notice of both the American Black masses and the Black masses who dwell within the African continent itself... No group is better positioned to launch this cultural revolution than India's Dalits. Since we form the foundation of this caste pyramid, we alone are capable of shaking its structure, if not demolishing it... The moment that our people come to believe that they are neither Hindus nor obligated to obey the upper castes, the whole caste structure completely collapses."

THE African PRESENCE IN EARLY JAPAN

The World of Sakanouye Tamuramaro: Black Shogun of Early Japan

According to the *Shoku Nihongi*, an official historical record, the Sakanouye clan is descended from Emperor Ling of the Chinese Han dynasty.[6][7] The Sakanouye clan's family tree shows that Tamuramaro is a 14th-generation descendant of Emperor Ling.[8

In the year 803 AD, Black Japanese General, Sakanouye no Tamuramaro, was beloved by all. This court noble, Shogun and minister of war for the Emperor of medieval Japan commanded his armies against the Emishi people to unify his island. This black Shogun was considered as a "paragon of military virtues". It was because of he this the Japanese proverb states, "For a Samurai to be brave, he must have a bit of black blood".

"In the first edition of the *Nations negres et culture* (1954), posited the hypothesis that the Yellow race must be the result of an interbreeding of Black and White in a cold climate, perhaps around the end of the Upper Paleolithic period. This idea is widely shared today by Japanese scholars and researchers. One Japanese scientist, Nobuo Takano, M.D., chief of dermatology at the Hammatsu Red Cross Hospital, has just developed this idea in Japanese that appeared in 1977,.

"Takano maintains, in substance, that the first human being was African/Black; then Africans gave birth to Whites, and the interbreeding of these two gave rise to the Yellow race; these three stages are in fact the title of his book in Japanese.

The first edition of the *Nations negres et culture* (1954), he posited the hypothesis that the Yellow race must be the result of an interbreeding of Black and White in a cold climate, perhaps around the end of the Upper Paleolithic period. This idea is widely shared today by Japanese scholars and researchers. One Japanese scientist, Nobuo Takano, M.D., chief of dermatology at the Hammatsu Red Cross Hospital, has just developed this idea in Japanese that appeared in 1977 Meaningful indications of an African presence in ancient Japan have been unearthed from the most remote ages of the Japanese past. To begin with, and as a significant example, a Feb. 15, 1986, report carried by the *Associated Press*

And we can cross the whole of Asia and find the African again, for when, in far-off Japan, the ancestors of the modern Japanese were

Revealing Unto the World, Bring Forth Clarity to Life, Who We Really Are, From Where do We Come & What Is Our Purpose

making their way northward against the Ainu, the aborigines of that country, the leader of their armies was Sakanouye Tamuramaro, a famous general and a African/Black."

Dr. W.E.B. DuBois (1868-1963), perhaps the greatest scholar in American history, in his book, The Negro (first published in 1915), placed Sakanouye Tamuramaro within a list of some of the most distinguished African rulers and warriors in antiquity. In 1922, Carter G. Woodson (1875-1950) and Charles Harris Wesley (1891-?) in a chapter called "Africans in History with Others," in their book The Negro in Our History, quoted Chamberlain on Tamuramaro verbatim. In the November 1940 issue of the Negro History Bulletin (founded by Dr. Woodson), artist and illustrator Lois Maillou Jones (1905-1998) contributed a brief article entitled "Sakanouye Tamura Maro." In the article Jones pointed out that:

"The probable number of Africans who reached the shores of Asia my be estimated somewhat by the wide area over which they were found on that continent. Historians tell us that at one time Negroes were found in all of the countries of southern Asia bordering the Indian Ocean and along the east coast as far as Japan. There are many interesting stories told by those who reached that distant land which at that time they called `Cipango.'

SOURCES: B

Chang, Kwan-chih. The Archaeology of Ancient China. New Haven: Yale University Press, 1963.

Chi, Li. The Formation of the Chinese People: An Anthropological Inquiry. 1928; rpt. New York: Russell and Russell, 1967.

Komaroff, Linda. Gifts of the Sultan. New Haven: Los Angeles County Museum of Art, Yale University Press, 2011.

Quartly, Jules. The Taipei Times, Nov. 27, 2004.

Rogers, J.A. Sex and Race, vol. 1. St. Petersburg: Helga M. Rogers, 1968.

The Los Angeles Times, Sept. 29, 1998.

Williams, Chancellor. The Destruction of Black Civilization. Chicago: Third World Press, 1976.

Chapter 6

───── ⌇⌇ ─────

Trip to China, tracing Her Family's Place of Birth

It was about that time in late Summer and just before the Fall season and semester were to begin. Chee had prep for the trip by buying appropriate clothing for the Chinese seasonal weather she would be experiencing. More importantly, the trio had achieved what they had set forth to do, is to gather the historical data records on the present of Africans early on in the Orient in ancient times BCE (Before the Common Era), which included not only China, but also Japan and India as well; their focus was on China in particular.

Chee was so overwhelmed by the share volume of informational data, the trio was able to obtain in such a limited time frame, of approximately two months. As such, she welcomed the opportunity to provide it to her immediate and extended family members, so they too, would feel part of her over all adventure, to their homeland of origin. The family couldn't fathom the facts, related to the Moorish African present, in the ancient Orient. Many of the family questioned the validity of the data references, but later would come to conceded, it was very likely to be mostly true, considering the outstanding source references, so highlighted!

There was much envy of Chee, having the chance to experience such an adventure, armed with this vast sources of archaeological and historical data, as reference points, to the places she would visit? It was pointed out, that she would likely be viewed as a outsider by the Chinese natives of the country, trying to spread information and knowledge they were not privilege to have learned in school? The Twins cautioned her, to limit her conversations to those she had developed a level of trust with; she in fact, would be residing in a communist country, as a invited student guest? Chee acknowledged, she would be very careful in what she said and the questions she would ask? That being said, the Twins had suggested, she should only use the newly uncovered data package as her personal reference point along the way?

Then the day came, for her departure at Kennedy International Airport. The plane was a Airbus A321LR, with long range capabilities, that would require only one stop for refueling. She had a window seat in the Coach section. The luggage compartments were limited and Chee only had the minimum carryon with her, she had planned to purchase gifts and some additional clothing while in China, that would reflect the trip. Weather in Beijing in the Autumn would likely be cool and with some precipitation; the temperature would mostly be comfortable, averaging in or about 15 degrees C/59 degrees F to 25 degrees C/77 degrees F.

Many of the family, immediate and extended, had taken time off, along with the Washington Twins, Tiye and Tarik, to see her safely off. The Twins felt a connection with Chee and wished they too could be on the Journey? They insisted that Chee take many photos and transmit them back electronically to both them and her family members! They asked Chee to FaceTime/chat them, when and if the opportunity presented itself?

Then it was time, as Chee had already board the plane, and the flight left the gate to taxi to its assigned runway. The giant twin engines

Revealing Unto the World, Bring Forth Clarity to Life, Who We Really Are, From Where do We Come & What Is Our Purpose

revved up glaring red with fire in the night darkness and there she went, high in the night sky; as the jetliner left at night, due to time zone differences. Everyone waved from the terminal, even though Chee, most likely, couldn't see them from the plane window seat, she was lucky to occupied.

The jetliner was slated to fly from JFK to China's Beijing Airport, via a stop over in Britain, at its Heathrow Airport. Estimated flight time was 17 hrs or so, before touch down at Beijing Airport, without any unanticipated problems, such as bad weather conditions and/or mechanical issues.

The Chinese University she was to attend, was in fact, in Beijing proper, therefore, the taxi ride to the campus dorms was relatively short, after more than 17 hrs in the air? The school had arranged to have a representative at the terminal, for the students arriving. There was several flight to come in, so after meeting up with the university representative, they waited around for the next few flights to arrive from different points of departure, because other colleges in the US also were participating in the program as well. Chee was excited to hear that news, that she would be able to mingle with other Americans on campus at certain times, if they weren't in the same classes?

Upon arrival on the campus, she was assigned a dorm room and the Chinese roommate, Shang Lee, who by the way, was well versed in both Chinese and English languages, keeping in mind, there are several Chinese dialects, which could likely present a problem on her exploratory trip to the Yellow River province in the countryside?

Her first week on campus was hectic, with the class assignments and getting oriented with locations of the medical buildings. Then came the class time, which was made easy, because her assigned roommate was on the same course track, so she shadowed Chee, in all her academic classes. It was the second week, that the US students got to socialize with each other for the first time. In fact, some even were in the same large lecture halls, that Chee was slated to attend.

One such US student was from Columbia also, even though they had never cross paths, back in New York on campus?Her name was Angie; they quickly befriended each other in the foreign environment.

Angie had frequented Chinese restaurants back in New York, but still wasn't familiar with some of the dishes severed in the Cafeteria, but Chee was, due to her Chinese heritage; she knew of most of the dishes, having been served them, by her Chinese relatives, at some point or another during her upbringing. This relationship with Angie was great; her family heritage was of an Italian and Irish American mix.

Well into the first months time, their relationship grew much closer naturally, and at that point, Chee was still undecided whether to share with Angie, the fact she was seeking to explore her African Chinese family connection?

Two more weeks pasted and at that time, Chee had come to have a higher level of confidence in Angie? She shared with her, that when they have midterm break, she intended to visit her family's places of birth, before they had migrated to the US. There would be logistical challenges to over-come, but she was determined to accomplish the task at hand! Angie was intrigued, so being somewhat curious, she asked if she could accompany Chee on the adventure; Chee said yes, why not, her company was welcomed! Angie asked if they could also visit the Great Wall, along the way and Chee said she would like that too? "China's Great Wall, UNESCO (United Nations Educational, Scientific and Cultural Organization) World Heritage Site".

Prior to the midterm break, Chee ask her roommate for help to lineup transportation to the Great Wall and the Yellow River province that her family came from. She explain to her, the deep desire to visit her family's birth place, where they have lived for years in China, before leaving for the US, where they currently resided. Her Chinese roommate, Shang, understood Chee's need, to experience both historical places, specifically where her family historically resided in China, at the Yellow River, for herself Her Chinese roommate, Shang, understood Chee's need, to experience both historical places, specifically where her family historically resided in China, at the Yellow River, for herself. It was a once in a lifetime opportunity and she needed to avail herself of this chance, to see for herself, the birth places of her Chinese heritage. Shang then suggested they take advantage of the two day weekend break, to visit each site on separate days, due to the travel distance between each; the two agreed on the suggestion Shang had made. Angie concurred, that the opportunity may only come once in a lifetime; Angie had yet to visit Italy or Ireland herself, the place of her family heritage and history?

With the help of Shang, the trip was plotted out over two days, first day to the near by Great Wall, and then the next day, onto the Yellow River.

The Mutianyu section of the Great Wall is located 73 kilometers (45 miles) from Beijing city center, taking 2 hours to get there by taxi. The driving distance between Beijing to Yellow River being noted as 446 km. It would take approximately 5 hour 17 minutes (Google Maps) to drive from Beijing to Yellow River. It would be a very long day, but an option of a two day trip, was plausible and it would allowed for more quality time for sightseeing?

Angie was so onboard with the taking of the trip in two days, not one, as originally planned, knowing that it would be some much more worth it, once in a lifetime for both her and classmate Chee. They were so excited to go on the midterm break weekend. The Saturday visit to the Great Wall, a "Wonder of the World", was very inspiring, as they walked some distance along the wall path, taking photos all along the way!

Upon their return to campus that day, neither could stop talking about the breath taking scenery along the Great Wall. The next morning trip to the Yellow River would be even more exciting, especially for Chee; neither could hardly wait as they return to their dorms to go to sleep! That Sunday morning was bright and sunny, and the women were both up and dressed early, ready to take the taxi, that Shang had arranged to travel to the Yellow River. They grabbed a quick snack in the cafeteria before, knowing the trip would take several hours. Their cellphones were fully charged overnight so they could take many pictures of the adventure!

Chee had previously taken video of the University campus and dorm room, along with photos of her roommate and fellow US classmates, like Angie, with her cellphone. It was not allowed by the Chinese government to transmit video or photos, via the TikTok internet connection, without authority granted by the government officials, assigned to the university campus? Chee and Angie would seek the required authorization later on during the semester? These restraints were explained to them both, during their the Chinese and Columbia University briefings, in an effort to properly prepare them for such communication guidelines constraints?

Chee was planning to share her family story with Angie, at some juncture, during the 5 hour trip to the Yellow River countryside, but only bits and pieces at a time, to determine what her reaction would likely be? What she did explain to Angie, is that her family was connected to Chinese ancient royalty, who once ruled the first initial dynasties of the land.

Angie was impressed, with Chee's Shang Dynasty royal blood connection, with past rulers of the land! About 2 hrs into the second leg of the trip, Chee ask Angie if she, had any prior knowledge of Chinese or African history; she replied, that her understanding was only superficial at best of either? Chee then explained further, that her best friends, the Washington Twins, Tiye and Tarik, help her do extensive research on both ancient Chinese and African history, well beyond the superficial level, in preparation for her trip to China, in order to expand her knowledge base and to allow her to be up to speed, in any event, as it related to her historical acknowledgment.

Angie couldn't understand, what was the significance of African history, as it related to this Chinese trip? She believed that Africans had no real history of note? It was at this point, she questioned Angie on her understanding of African explorers and rulers of foreign lands? It was then, Angie, a learned Pre-Med student, exhibited her ignorance of any legitimate African historical facts. She was schooled to believe, the peoples of Africa were merely slaves, brought to the Americas and other places in the world, to serve as slaves and therefore had no historical significance, prior to that, which impacted on world empires, in anyway or fashion; they had no culture of note!

Chee went on to explain to Angie how the Twins had enlightened her and their schoolmates as well, of the hidden greatness of the Africans of Kemet(Greek termed Egypt) and the Moorish population of Northern Africa. Her first response was obviously programmed, when she implied, that those people were not African(Black), but some mixture of an Arabic cultures/backgrounds? Chee, when on to explain further, that the translation of the name Kemet, means "Land of the Black"; it was the Greeks who call the African Empire "Egypt". She then presented to Angie, the research package, that was put together by her and the twins over the summer, prior to the trip?

Once the initial shock wore off, only after her review of the significant research data and references documented credentials. Angie, then had to conceded, she was totally ignorant of these facts, because her rich and privileged, Bergen county New Jersey suburban education, neglected to provided her with a truly legitimate representation of the global history? This was somewhat of an embarrassment to her, that she had in fact, been so short changed of facts, intentionally hidden for political and power controlling reasons, in connection with world dominance? Angie, at that point, was in a state of mind that apparently couldn't accept that Chee, as a person of Asian heritage, which did factually included a 20% African bloodlines linkage? The ancestral research indicated that the many of the Chinese population exhibited that same 1/5 th % DNA bloodline; that most, were without the awareness of their true African connective relationship?

Angie, was again, placed back into a state of shock and some dismay, but was slowly beginning to come to an understanding of the facts and data provided to her; keeping in mind, Angie was a STEM/ STEAMM (Science, Technology, Engineering, Art, Mathematics & Medicine) student of high intelligence and IQ, as had been demonstrated academically, over her scholastic years. It was Chee's data on Ancestral documented DNA studies and scientific examinations of ancient skeletal remains, in conjunction with ancient writing, found by world's renowned archeologists, that apparently sealed the deal of belief, on the part of Angie, at least on a temporary basis, which likely was only superficially?

The taxi limo, arranged by Shang, had arrived at the Yellow River site and Chee and Angie got out to begin the exploratory adventure. She was overcome by the mere thought she was walking on the soil of her ancestral origin, where the Luang linage had its historical beginning!

It was unbelievable that Chee had finally made this connection on a physical basis; she was hardly able to wrap her head around the experience! She immediately began documenting the visit on video to share, back home with family and friends.

On the ride back to campus, Chee asked Angie not to reveal to others on campus, any of the information she was so kind to share, because they were now in fact, in a Communist environment and they wanted no possibility of trouble that might result, if others knew of Chee's heritage, most often not known by indigenes Chinese, because their government didn't want them to be made aware of the significant African historical connection; keeping in mind, the Western educational institutions never had revealed that same information to their student body either?

Prior to the trip, the Columbia University had briefed the student group on the specific behavior to be conducted in a communist

Revealing Unto the World, Bring Forth Clarity to Life, Who We Really Are, From Where do We Come & What Is Our Purpose

country, as invited guests; they certainly didn't want the students to become political prisoners, because they mistakenly violated the expected protocol. It should be pointed out, the US State Department was hands-on in all of the preparatory briefing guidelines. Each student was required to sign an agreement, stating that they would adhere to the Chinese government behavioral guidelines and protocol. Chee and Angie both, made certain that the photos and videos they had taken at the Great Wall and the Yellow River, were none controversial, nor government military sensitive, in anyway?

After returning to the school campus each day, Chee and Angie's cellphone videos and photos were checked, before they were authorized for transmitted to their families back in the states. The Chinese officials had to disengage the highly sophisticated TikTok electronic firewall barrier, which prohibited the transmission of unauthorized cellphone data, I.E. all video and photo electronic context, had to first be vetted and authorized by the government officials, before outside internet transmission could ever take place?

After the midterm break concluded, it was back to the business of school; both Chee and Angie both did very well on their midterm exams across the board. With no further breaks scheduled, the two students kept a low profile and prioritize the academic aspects of the stay; determined to achieving excellent final grade point averages?

Before they knew it, their overseas exchange students semester had concluded. Both women were so glad they were able to share the experience together and how that encouraged them, to obtain such high grade point averages as a result. They reminisced about the rare times they had to socialize during the semester, but the Great Wall and Yellow River trips were always the highlight! Neither had shared the details of their adventure with anyone on campus and certainly not with anyone back in the states, via text or/and during monitored phone conversations. Each student was allowed just two phone calls to their family members, during the five month semester?

Angie's flight plans home were somewhat different from Chee's;

the flight from Beijing to London's Heathrow Airport, was luckily the same, but Angie would disembark in London, to then board her flight, destined for Newark International Airport, near her Bergen County New Jersey home; while Chee would stay onboard, continuing on to New York's JFK Airport, where her family awaited her, in anticipation of her return home! All went well and the young ladies both reached there destinations safe and sound! Before parting company in London, both Angie and Chee promised to stay in contact and reconnect during their Spring semester on the Columbia University campus; it was there, they could finally have a detailed discussion about the midterm trip to the Great Wall and more importantly, to the Yellow River; Chee's family quest for closure on her newly discovered African bloodlines?

Chapter 7

RECLAMATION OF GLOBAL WISDOM AND ACKNOWLEDGEMENT

THIS IS WHERE the discussion turns to determining the lasting impact on Chee's personality and how she would process and cope, in the present and future, with what she now knew to be true, about herself, via the legitimate family hereditary bloodlines; will she be a better person, now knowing that there is an African connection in her Chinese culture and more importantly, directly with her Shang royal family line?

What video and photos Chee was allow to transmit back to the family, were so very appreciated by each and everyone; they understood, there was a government limit on the number of photos and length of the videos, put into place, by the Chinese government officials; her mom, dad, sister and brother all, treasured them, never the less. Both of the children hoped someday to have a similar opportunity, to visit their homeland of China as well? The plan was to have the electronic photos printed and placed in picture fames, so they could be proudly displayed, on the walls of their home!

Chee asked her parents, if she could share both the same videos and photos with her friends, the T & T Washington Twins, they replied certainly, they had played such a vital role in the preparation for the venture, in the first place! By the way, Chee needed to give them a call, to let them know, she was back from her Chinese trip!

The twins were so excited to hear Chee's voice over phone, they immediately placed her on speaker, during the phone call. Chee gave them a condensed summary of the trip, but promised to send to them the videos and photos taken; at some point in time, they would meet up to get a more detail summary of the adventure. Chee did informed them that, the historical facts and data package, they all put together, came in handy in so many ways! The conversation then concluded, by establishing a tentative date to get together, in person, before each of their Spring semesters would commence!

With not much time to collect her thoughts, Chee could never conceive of having never taken the trip? It was apparent, that she would never again be the same person, before getting to know she had a legitimate genetic African connection. For certain, Chee's global historical cultural views and thoughts were forever altered in a positive fashion. She was made more aware of the racial and cultural connectivity that all peoples share! What she was unable to convey, while in China, was the appreciation and respect, she now enjoyed for African peoples and their under recorded accomplishments and achievements, over the millenniums of the human timeline. What was impressive, was how she was comfortable in sharing the African data and facts, with an unbeliever and uninformed, fellow American, like Angie? A person, like her, so mis-informed and racialize, via an intentional inadequate educational curriculum and syllabus, designed to Westernize all students to accept, as fact, that European supremacy and privilege was normal and should be accepted, without question? As a person of science and medicine, she knew, going forward, never to believe something that everyone apparently acknowledged as truth, because it can be such a false narrative, politically and cultural motivated, put into place to control and manipulate the masses. She, in fact, wanted to follow up with Angie on campus, at some point, to determine if she, in deed, still had any doubts about the positive influences of Africans, on the cultures and societies, all across the globe, in deed, even in Europe proper, where her family originated?

It was the Moors, that precisely had defined European society for the better part of a millennium (711 – 1492 AD), while controlling Spain and Portugal on the Iberian peninsula!

They had established worlds first public education, libraries, cuisine, universities, architecture, art, etc.. It was the Moors, in fact, who trigger the Renaissance of Europe (15th – 16th Centuries), in large part, which followed after the Moors were defeated in Spain in 1492 AD. Much of this and more was never taught to Chee and others like her, and having yet to appear in the mainstream text books in the education systems around this globe, in the 21st century; due in large part, of the dominance of Eurocentric thought!

In summary, the reader needs to decide, if Chee has made a true transformation or not? Any transformation, would have be accompanied by an actual conscious revision, and questioning of Western thinking, and dominance going forward? Given the existing worlds paradigm and parameters, that govern the societal and cultural environments of the 21st century, nothing of this kind is a certainty? With consciousness, along with awaken thought, we are all caught in a state of being, a daily work in progress. Who you surround yourself with, along with, what type of factors that influence your thoughts, and establishes one's state of mind, sets the tone. The dynamics are fluid and must be reenergize along the way, in order to supersede the apparent overwhelming dominance inter-structure, currently in place? It should be noted that the apparent state of dominance, is somewhat on the decline, on so many levels, how this process continues to waver, certainly will take a considerable amount of time, to convince the disbelievers, for sure? I leave you with this thought, keep an open mind and fact check everything and everyone, no matter who they may be; that certainly includes my works as well! No one is correct a 100% of the time, think for yourself, never conceding that task to the so called designated societal and intellectual experts! As the T &T Twins, Tiye and Tarik, had so wisely informed Chee Luang, that her journey was a spiritual one, akin to the African Sankofa Holy Ghost experience, that is now embedded in her DNA; it had always resided there, but not to her acknowledgement or state of her conscious awareness? This experience had truly resurrected the African component of her spiritual inheritance. She was now aware that Africans, in large part, are the mothers and fathers of all of global humanity!

"Africans are the Root/Origin of the Human Genome."

It is her birthright, to now truly take on ownership of her ability to fully control the flight of her life's quest; to then find her designated purpose, with a legitimate understanding of who she really is and what she is destined to achieve, in making the world a better place, than when she found it, upon her birth arrival on earth. A flying young eagle must soar to live! Both her Chinese and African spiritual consciousness, will guide her, as she now continues the life journey. She has now acknowledged that "Man/Women Must Know Themselves", as so stated by the world first multi genius, the African, Imhotep! Chee now knows she can call on both, Chinese wisdom from Confucius and that of the African genius, Imhotep.

It was truly a miracle, she made the African connection via her Sankofa experience; others should perhaps consider taking on their own unique search and discovery of their family ancestral roots, so many have forgotten or never knew? Let it be known, that we are all connected in one way or another! This can only result in one coming to empowerment of their true inner self!

Chapter 8

───❧───

READER DOCUMENT THOUGHTS AND FEEDBACK, (4 BLANK LINED PAGES)

Reader Thoughts and Feedback Lined PCF Pages #56:

_____
_____
_____
_____
_____
_____
_____
_____
_____
_____

Reader Thoughts and Feedback Lined PCF Pages #58:

_____

Reader Thoughts and Feedback Lined PCF Pages #59:

Reader Thoughts and Feedback Lined PCF Pages #60:

Chapter 9

REFERENCE AND
RESEARCH SOURCES

Books and Reference resource material list; sources of learning, knowledge and full understanding. These are portal sources of intellectual and academic data and facts often hidden in an attempt to erase the true historical data/facts of the peoples of color of humanity.

1. "The Lies My Teacher Told Me" by James Loewe
2. PBS DVD "Africa's Great Civilizations" by Prof. Henry Louis Gates
3. "The First Americans Were Africans" by Prof. David Imhotep Ph.D
4. "Black Athena" by Martin Bernal
5. "Great African Thinkers" by Ivan Van Sertima
6. "The Destruction Of Black Civilization" by Prof. Chancellor Williams
7. "The African Origin Of Civilization" by Cheikh Anta Diop
8. "Black Spark White Fire" by Richard Poe
9. "The Moors After Spain" by Stanley Lane-Poole

10. "The Black Discovery Of American ".by Michael Bradley

11. "Before The Mayflower" by Lerone Bennett Jr.

12. "Egypt Before The Pharaohs" by Michael A. Hoffman

13. "They Came Before Columbus" by Ivan Van Sertima

14. CD "Ancient African History" 1 & 2 by Dr. John Henrik Clark & Dr. Ben—Jochannan

16. DVD "A Great and Mighty Walk" by Dr. John Henrik Clark

17. "Between The World And Me" by Ta-Nehisi Coates

18. "Before the Mayflower, A History Of Black America" by Lerone Bennett Jr.

19. "The Negro Impact On Western Civilization" by Joseph S. Boucek & Thomas Kiernan

20. "Black Achievement" by Margaret Peters

21. "Blacks In Science (ancient and modern)" by Ivan Van Sertima

22. "NEA Today, Let's Talk About Race"; How Racism's stubborn Roots in Public Schools Affect You And Your Students.—October 2019 magazine issue

23. "Countering The Conspiracy To Destroy Black Boys" four book series by educator Jamanza Kunjufu

24. "Light From Ancient Africa" by Na'im Akbar, Ph.D.

25. "The Prince" by Machiavelli

26. "Lincoln's Code" by John Fabian Witt

27. "The 1619 Project" by Nikole Hannah—Jones

28. "See Us, From Whence We Come" by R. E. Vincent Daniels*

29. "Truth Awakens, Daring To Dream Of Past Glory In Order To Envision Future Greatness" by R. E. Vincent Daniels *.

30. "Igniting the Fire, Brings the Light, From Invisibility to Academic Viability and Excellence" by R. E. Vincent Daniels *

* Note: Recommended prerequisites to first read books 28, 29 & 30 in order to place one's thoughts and/or comment feedback into a realistic context and prospective! One must be of the mind set to be able to "Connect The Dots".

These books are Graphic Nobels currently in print and are available on several major platforms and search engines Google & EBay. Barnes & Noble site.

Simply click on this link to view.
"https://www.barnesandnoble.com/.../see-us-r.../1136948748...".

T site.

Simple click on the link below for all details & status:
"http://www.amazon.com/dp/B08999NSY8".

Walmart Books site;

simple click on the link below for details.
https://www.google.com/url?sa=t&rct=j&q=&esrc=s&source=web&cd=&ved=2ahUKEwi0kbr5nLr3AhUqpIkEHQq2BXYQFnoECAgQAQ&url=https%3A%2F%2Fwww.walmart.com%2Fip%2FSee-Us-From-Whence-We-Come-Paperback-9781977224200%2F373203257&usg=AOvVaw0cXh8qrFXjgmaEDpv8D4K8